JOHN E. COCKAYNE, JR.

# Into Your Hands, Lord

To _____    From _____

On the occasion of _____

# INTO YOUR HANDS, LORD

## Dom Helder Camara

### Translated by Robert R. Barr

MEYER STONE BOOKS

Translated from the Portuguese *Em tuas mãos, Senhor!*, in the collection "A oração dos pobres" directed by José Comblin, Carlos Mesters, and Maria Emília Ferreira, and published by Edições Paulinas, Rua Dr. Pinto Ferraz, 183, 04117 São Paulo, SP, Brazil. Copyright © 1986 Edições Paulinas.

The Foreword by José Comblin has been extracted and translated by John Eagleson from "Dom Helder e o novo modelo episcopal do vaticano II," in *Dom Helder, Pastor e Profeta*, Edições Paulinas, São Paulo, 1984. Used with permission.

"Dom Helder Camara Speaks to His Flock" has been extracted from Dom Helder Camara's inaugural address to the diocese of Olinda and Recife, Brazil, April 12, 1964, published in English as "Dom Helder Camara introduces himself to his flock" in *Church and Colonialism*, Sheed and Ward, London, 1969. Translated by William McSweeney. Used with permission.

Manufactured in the United States of America

91  90  89  88  87          5  4  3  2  1

Meyer-Stone Books ISBN 0-940989-06-9

Cover and text design by Evans-Smith & Skubic, Inc.

Illustration by Timothy Whitney Desley.

Jesus cried out in a loud voice,
"Father! Into your hands
I place my spirit!"
—Luke 23:46

# Contents

# Dom Helder—
## Gospel Messenger

One of the characteristics of Dom Helder's preaching has
been its universality. He has never preached for Catholics
only. His words, his gestures, his personality have generated
as much enthusiasm among non-Catholics as among
Catholics, and at times even more among the non-Catholics.
He is the only Catholic bishop who has had a true audience
in the non-Catholic world. For many he has been the image
of the Catholic bishop, for they have had no other. Most
other bishops are not even known by their names.

Dom Helder has been the St. Paul of our day, the apostle
to the "pagans," the apostle to the outside world. Some
2,000 bishops evangelize the world of the present-day
"Jews," and one, like Paul, has evangelized the Gentiles.
The Vatican intervened, forcing Dom Helder to limit his
trips abroad—a limitation that Peter did not impose on
Paul; but over the centuries the system has been "perfected."
Dom Helder was obedient and submitted to the restrictions
on his evangelizing activity. Some accused him of abandoning
or neglecting his diocese. In a church in which some 2,000
bishops administer their respective territories, couldn't one
of them evangelize the world? A bishop, like any Christian,
is above all an apostle sent to the world.

Some believe that Dom Helder did not give sufficient
attention to the development of the pastoral institutions
that were advocated by the Second Vatican Council. This
may be so; let those who know the secrets of administration
pronounce judgment.

After the Council of Trent in the sixteenth century the
bishop was above all responsible for the rigorous and literal

3

application of the canons of reform of the Council. He was a fiscal officer, an inspector. His job was to monitor all the doctrines taught in his diocese, the administration of the sacraments, and all the expressions of worship, to monitor with zeal the conduct of the priests, to assure order in the parishes and the convents, and to watch over the records of the baptized, the confirmed, and the dead. He was even responsible for the accounting of souls, monitoring the behavior of each of the faithful.

It seems that Dom Helder did not conform to this model, and thousands of complaints must have reached the Vatican, listing the faults, abuses, and errors present in his diocese. In today's circumstances would a diocese be more effective if the rigorous monitoring of the Council of Trent model were practiced? We needn't reject the model of the careful administrator, but it is difficult to find, in a single person, all the features corresponding to such different missions.

Beyond models, no one will deny that Dom Helder had an original and inimitable way of being bishop. It was not just that he wore his cassock in every country and circumstance. It was not just his facility of expression, the special look of the room he lives in, his ability to live while eating hardly at all. There are many other dimensions to Dom Helder that fit into no analysis, for they belong to no model at all. A personality like Dom Helder's cannot be boxed within a model. He could not have imitators and, as a personality, he will have no successors. In this sense his successor will have no problems. Since imitation is impossible, comparisons will not be made.

Like all apostles in the history of the church, Dom Helder has repeated always and untiringly the same message. He has had a single message, and that message is what the world has awaited from him. When he arrives in a country, everybody knows what he is going to say, and it is precisely that message that challenges our times. Dom Helder does not speak of the needs or problems of the church, but rather addresses the word of Jesus to the pagan world in a form that that world can understand.

Some have said that his message is not "religious." But neither was the message of Jesus. Justice and dignity for the masses of the Third World—is that not the message of Jesus? That is why the world listens to Dom Helder and wants him to repeat unceasingly the same message. For no one else can proclaim the message with the authority that Dom Helder does.

It was many years ago that Dom Helder first set out as a pilgrim of the Third World. For years he has been in communication with many peoples. Not everyone understands his chaotic English nor his foreign French, but everyone understands his gestures, his personality, and his message. We all know that in the relationship between a leader and the leader's group, speeches are worth little. The group listens to the music of the speeches, but is not concerned with the words. The group understands what the speaker wants to say better than the speaker can express it. This is the case with Dom Helder.

Dom Helder is better known today outside Brazil than within the country. Countless groups are named after him, in all the accents of the world. Universities grant him doctoral degrees honoris causa, not to honor him but to have the honor of listing him among their Ph.D.'s. They would be embarrassed not to have him included. Even the Brazilian universities have felt obliged to grant him the same title—to avoid ridicule.

There is no use to studying the "doctrine" of Dom Helder Camara. There is no doctrine of Saint Francis of Assisi, nor of Saint Francis Xavier, nor of the missionaries of the sixteenth century. What matters is the gospel, the message ever repeated, with distinct variations, but ever the same.

José Comblin

# Into Your Hands, Lord

# Deus é Amor

Fomos nós, as tuas Criaturas
que inventámos teu nome !?...
O nome não é,
não pode, não deve ser
um rótulo colado
sobre as pessoas e sobre as coisas...
O nome vem de dentro
das coisas e pessoas,
e não deve soar falso...
Tem que exprimir
o mais íntimo do íntimo,
a própria razão
de ser e de existir
da coisa ou da pessoa nomeada...
Teu nome
é e só podia ser
Amor!....

+Helder Câmara

# God is Love

Is it for us, your creatures,
to suit a name to you?

A name is not a label
stuck
on persons or things.

A name has to well from within
and ring true!
A name must surge
from the within of the within.
A name must emerge
to cry
the *raison d'être*
*et d'existir*
of a thing or person
*with a name.*

Ah, then your name
is ...
can only be ...
Love.

# The first time ...

... your name sprang forth
was before time,
amidst eternity—
when from everlasting
you knew yourself
and your self-knowing
generated
your Divine Son.

And when from everlasting,
Father and Son
were face to face—
one and couple—
the Holy Spirit
in perfect oneness
consummated the Trinity.

In this eternal instant,
before, beyond time,
your name rolled through the abyss:
Love!

# Love poured out

With the Most Holy Trinity
love's potential
for infinite manifestations
was exhausted for good and all.

You knew
beyond the shadow of a doubt
that a creation,
a thing beyond yourself,
must inescapably be
finite, imperfect, bounded.

Yet you created.
And creation—
for all its bounds,
its imperfections,
its finitude—
is far from being the burgeoning
of a love not really genuine, some love not true!

Far from springing
from a false love,
all things you have created—
for those with ears to hear—
tingle with the echo
of Love
pure and infinite!

# What humility ...

... and audacity
you reveal in your creation—
in the beyond-God!
Supreme perfection
creates the imperfect.
The infinite
creates the finite,
the fleeting,
the bounded.

But your humility
soared to its summit
when you exalted
one creature—
your human creature—
to the responsibility
and glory
of your image and likeness,
with the charge to subdue nature:
to finish creation!

Yes, behold the echo
of Love ultraterrestrial
and ultrahumane,
for those who have ears to hear:
in the beating
of the human heart.

# What is love, for you?

Yourself—
the presence of you
cloaking the universe from end to end,
animating and transfiguring!

All nature learns your love.
Yet none but the human creature
is possessed of the conditions,
so special,
for learning Love by loving:
Thanks to you
the human heart,
whenever it loves,
thirsts for the infinite,
everlasting
absolute.

Love, touch us.
Give us to feel your infinite Love
as you bestow it on us—
and as it leaves us needy and poor!
For now we stand in need of human love.
To love you, to love Love itself,
is to devote our lives
to the Amorization
of the universe.

# Anti-love: selfishness

Anti-love is selfishness,
closure, seclusion
within oneself,
that renders all encounter
with anyone at all
impossible.
Anti-love ...
... is the Sevenfold Selfishness,
Egoism of the seven masks:

Wrath and fury, hate and frigidity, jealousy.
Envy, our shame, that we so dislike to confess.
Greed—and not just for gold! (Far from it.
   A greed for love is the most pitiable of all.)
Gluttony—by no means
   the affair of food and drink alone.
Lust, that demeans the human body
   beneath the false cloak of love.
Sloth, by which we lay our own burden
   on the backs of others.
Pride and conceit—more than anything else
   a failing in intelligence,
   and blindness
   to the ridiculous.

Those who think they love
and love to tell you
love the least.
Deep down
they love only
themselves.

They do not even know
what love is.

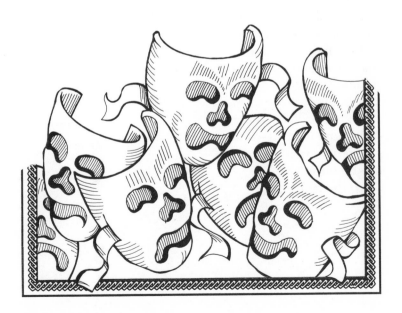

# Enroll us in your school of love

Teach us to love and be loved,
in perfect transparency.

Let our love be diaphanous,
lest we project
the mote in our eye
into the eye of another,
and make it a beam besides!

Let our love be transparent,
lest we ever play host
to a love that is false.
Love that springs from aught but you,
love that lives in aught but you,
love that returns not to you,
is not love.

Teach us to love each and every person
as if he or she
were the only person on earth.
After all,
this is how you love:
uniquely, truly, robustly,
and perfectly, with your own perfection.

In us,
in this poor human clay,
love creates incredible problems.
Our *machismo* knows no bounds,
engulfing all three sexes,
and most cruelly
the third.

# When your boundless love …

… impels the human heart,
we marvel.
How come these narrow frontiers
to embrace
One that knows no bounds?

Ah, but more mysterious still,
and defiant of all penetration:
How come we to fly so low
when the currents under our wings
are none other than the puffs
vast and mighty
that your Spirit alone can breathe!

# Who is the poorest of the poor?

The one without silver?
   Without a roof?
   Without work?
   Without health?

Is not the poorest of the poor
the one
without love?

But there is more.
Those men or women
who will not love,
turn where they may,
and beckon who might—
these will be not only unloving,
but unlovable!

The deepest penury of all—
   the saddest, the most wrenching—
   despite all appearances—
is that of one who has not Love
   to give,
   to spread,
   to sow!

# Breathes there a fleshly love that you would scorn?

You are the Creator of life.

A child is born.
How foolish we should be
to think "God's part" the soul alone,
the deathless spirit you create
and craft so fine
to the measure of the shoot
that sprouts in the maternal womb
the moment both seeds of life,
the mother's and the father's,
meet, embrace, fuse.

The human body
is your creation too!
It would never exist
save for the breath of love
breathed from your lips.

And it is the whole body
from head to toe
that receives your breath.
The human body has no shameful parts—
no parts uncreated by you!
Were sheer nakedness evil, immoral,
then surely God
would cause
babies to be born
in breechcloths!

The human body, whole and entire,
not only receives a spirit—
that soul created for it by you ...

The human body
is the living temple
of the Holy Trinity.

# And once more ...

... do you forbid, condemn,
carnal love?
The flesh, the human body,
forms, in your divine plan,
a unity
with that fresh creation of yours,
the human soul.

If a woman or man
live life to the full,
the body of such a one at every moment
manifests the soul.
   The look, the gaze,
   the hands,
   the smile,
   the gait—
   how many bodily manifestations!—
render the soul
all but visible to the naked eye.

The kiss
of that woman or man
who knows how to echo the spirit, the soul,
in all of life
is but the flower of that soul and spirit
hastening to the lips to bloom.

Meeting of lips,
souls' embrace.
Provided only
fullness of life reign

in these lovers.
A body burns
for the touch of another ...
Ah, the encounter of spouses,
the fusion of bodies,
will be perfect
if a fusion of souls
has gone before.
For then ...

... The Book of Genesis
is written all over again
in two hearts.

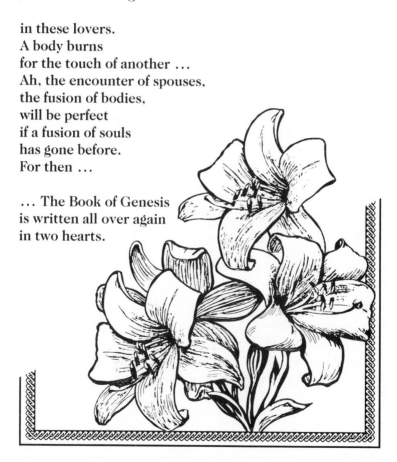

# When the human creature
# that we are ...

... is too solicitous
for the body,
wasting time
and spending money
(how much of each!)
for the restoration of the facade—
to the total,
or nearly,
neglect of the spirit—
then the most it can hope for
is a beauty quenched,
lusterless within.

But a restoration of the soul—
now, that is a different matter!
A soul restored
will manage the transfiguration
not only of a body with a blemish,
but of a body however misshapen and crippled!

# Blessed are they who discover ...

... besides physical relaxations,
spiritual ones.

Oh, I know,
when the body lies abed and slumbers,
the spirit also rests.
Such, after all, is the composition
of the human unity.
But there are recreations
specific to the spirit.
Would you know a few? ...

Immersion in nature,
music, a chat with friends—
or, when you have the happiness of believing,
a chat with God,
which has no need of words ...

As bodily repose
redounds to the spirit's rest,
so too does spiritual refreshment
revitalize (more than I can say!)
Brother Body.

# Aren't you going too far, Lord …

… with your respect for human freedom?

Your love extends to all creatures.

But you reserve your special love
for the small, the simple, the poor.
Then how can you bear to see
these millions,
your daughters and sons,
living in conditions less than human,
simply through the selfishness,
the ambition,
the injustice
of minorities oppressing them?

You cannot be oblivious
of your cataclysms and catastrophes—
　　flood and drought,
　　volcano spewing,
　　pitiless windstorm,
　　the earth quaking and tumbling—
Why must these
strike down the littlest ones of all,
the ones whose life
is already beneath human dignity
without your catastrophes.
Is it not enough that they be crushed
by disease, or human frailty?

What explanation can there be
for all you send?

Is the only answer
we may know,
and all we need to know:

that you grant human beings intelligence,
and teach them to overcome
nature's disasters?

# Your Son has taught us …

… that any who would follow him
must day by day
take up a cross—
his or her own cross—
then follow.

Are love and suffering,
love and the cross,
therefore the same?
Do these converge,
and merge,
fuse in one?

We cannot say.
But this we know,
for we live it:
When cross
and cross alone
falls on our shoulders
it crushes us to earth
and shreds us to the winds.
But when
the cross comes
with Christ …
we have his kiss!

# Amorization

Amorization! Amorization!
Let us have a new word.
Let us derive it from amor,
love.

Love is God. God is love.
God is love!
Amorization is the mission God entrusts
to one who loves Love.

To one who loves Love!
    The one who welcomes love's assault,
    muscle to muscle, nerve to nerve—
    the one who welcomes love's assault,
    the one who welcomes God's assault,
    has grown enough—
    to begin to amorize.

The soil is readied,
    the seed is selected,
        the garden is watered,
           and it trembles
               with the sprouting
                  of love's first shoots.

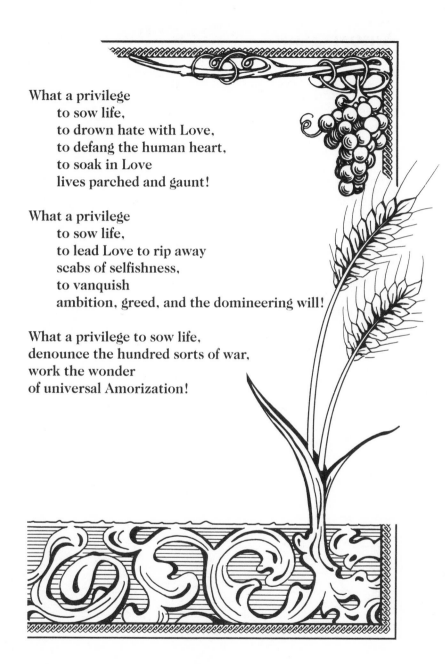

What a privilege
    to sow life,
    to drown hate with Love,
    to defang the human heart,
    to soak in Love
    lives parched and gaunt!

What a privilege
    to sow life,
    to lead Love to rip away
    scabs of selfishness,
    to vanquish
    ambition, greed, and the domineering will!

What a privilege to sow life,
denounce the hundred sorts of war,
work the wonder
of universal Amorization!

# Master means Lord and Ruler ...

... and mistress means Lady: lady who reigns.
Ah, would the Lords and Ladies of this earth
but live their names,
those beautiful names,
and love their subjects,
who depend on them!

Terrible is the deed of those
who read love as dominion,
and seek to lord it over,
to tyrannize,
the persons
bound to them!

# What is mine is yours ...

... and what is yours, mine.

Empty words.
Unless
   beforehand
   we live
   the interrelationships
   that in the Holy Trinity
   are sheerest reality:

"I am what you are,
and you are what I am!"

# Teach me, Good Samaritan ...

... to lead
trampled hearts,
crushed souls,
victims robbed of their spirit.

It were best
you spoke no word,
but purely,
simply,
suffered
with them.

# The baby

The baby with her tiny steps
needs to scamper a bit
from time to time
to keep pace
with grownups ...

Just so, my God—
how often you take me in your arms
to spare me the embarrassment
of looking like a turtle!

# My friend had four little ones ...

... and oh! how attentively they listened
as I told them,
once again:
"This box of candy
is for you four, all four—
one; two,
three, four.
Do you understand?"
Four nods.

And I handed the box
to the very littlest.
But not without a reminder
that the candy was for all four.

The little boy
clutched the box to his breast,
exclaiming,
"It's mine!
It's mine!"

And I thought:
My goodness.
One would think one were attending
a meeting
of heads of state.

# The day draws near …

… when we humans
will find
the reins of nature's forces.
That day we shall speed through space.
And there
amidst worlds of worlds,
suns and their planets, millions,
billions of times our little earth,
we shall be able
at last
to form a more realistic estimate
of God's greatness
and the comic absurdity
of human pride.

Even our wars
will seem wars of
not ants
but earthworms!

# How often, as a child …

… I rushed after the horizon,
to find where earth and sky,
or sky and sea,
link arms!

But I always returned with my thirst
unslaked,
multiplied by
infinity.

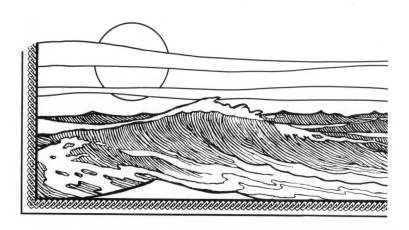

# Which is worse ...

... to relativize the absolute,
or absolutize the relative?

Well, at all events
we can rest assured
that there exists but one Absolute
really:
God!

# It is all very well …

… to plunge headlong
into unbridled sexual license.
Yes, and laugh at romanticism,
and consider yourself
totally free
of "foolish emotions"
and "silly sentimentalism."

But one day love
will strike you down with all its might.
Terrified,
you will cry out
from your inmost depths:

   "You shall be mine
   forever
   and ever!"

# The Creator has kindled in us …

… a thirst for perfection—
for the absolute,
for the infinite,
for immortality.

Then why does perfection
escape us?

Why does it melt like a mirage
in the very moment
of our certitude
that we have created it, attained it?

To punish our measureless ambition?

No.
To spur us
never
to feel smug, content—
satisfied!

# The Father of Heaven smiled …

… when his Divine Son
established for us
his standard of perfection:
To be perfect
as his Father and ours.

Never could Christ have found
a more convincing way
to prove to us
that, in the matter of perfection,
no one, no one, no one
can sit down,
and feel arrived—
feel at the summit,
presume a right to rest!

# Suddenly you learn …

… your health is gone.
Happy are those
who, when that moment comes,
will be found so well prepared by grace
that they accept this suffering,
really,
as a rich gift of God,
and death,
really,
as the beginning
of True Life,
endless Life!

# Lord, you hardly need …

… gasps and cries of mine
("Lord, do you see?" I say,
for fear you don't!)
to teach you what you know:

    Worse than a prison
    where only a narrow,
    oh! so narrow
    ray of light
    pierces the empty gloom—

are lives
compressed and crushed—
so little air
or brightness within
that one could despair
of ever entering there
or doing aught.

# Celebrating the Holy Sacrifice ...

... I hesitated.
Could I say
that the Offering I would make to you
was "perfect"?
But the true Celebrant
is ever
your divine Son.
So I took heart
and breath and cried,
yes, "... *Perfect* offering,
Sacrifice of *life and holiness!*"

And even through the day,
far from your altar,
but still at *one* with your divine Son,
I make a *perfect offering* in every instant,
a *full and holy consecration*
that transfigures all,
anticipating life eternal—
and celebrate a *Communion*
that envelops, embraces all,
excluding nothing,
excluding no one.

# Father in Heaven ...

Thank you ...
    The agitation of the day is done,
        and you send us the repose of night ...
            How blessed the peace of the night,
                so still
                    that the very stones
                        of mountain, of skyscraper,
                            lose their jutty, harsh aspect,
                            and bathe in thrilling
                                stillness.

Let us not ruminate
    the disagreeable scenes of the day ...
        Let us not rehearse
            injustices,
                bitter, hard words,
                    coarse acts.

Mindful, Father,
    of your infinite patience with us,
        your infinite goodness,
            we ask you to help us
                never to harbor so much as a thimbleful
                    of hatred, or resentment,
                  or bitterness
                    against anyone
                      whomsoever ...

Fill us
    with your mercy,
        your limitless mercy.
            Amen.

# Oh, Lord, I admit …

… that, by your grace,
I could thank you for, and love,
any corner of the earth
in which I had first seen light.

Will it come as a shock to you, then,
to hear my thanks,
my special thanks,
for having been born in Ceará?

Do you know
I have to be on my guard
against a certain temptation to vanity,
a certain pride that's—
no one's monopoly, of course, but—
really rather *cearense*
no matter how you look at it?

Will you be astonished, Father,
to hear me say—
or will this be old news for you?—
that one of the deepest reasons
I love the Land you have chosen for me
is that to this day
I know not
whether a *cearense*
would prefer to bend
without breaking,
or break without bending?
(Well, both, actually!)

# Oh, I know you are spirit ...

... and have no body, as we, or as your Son,
who by the action of the Divine Spirit
took
in Mary's womb
a body like our own ...

But the one who first cried
*In manus tuas,*
"Into your hands ..."
was Christ on the cross.

Then have you hands?
What, in you,
amounts to, transcends infinitely,
the protection of hands?

I swear ...
that ever more and more,
yes, ever more,
I feel myself to be a baby bird
cupped
in the hollow of your hand!

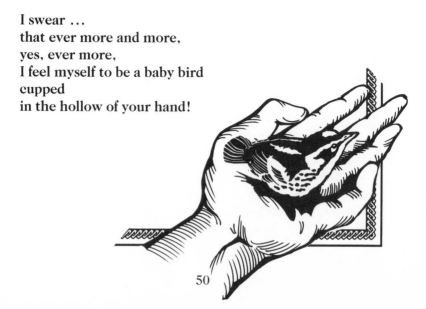

# Charity is Love ...

... and Love is you, Lord God!
Charity is infinite as you ...
so infinite
that each new generation
can only hope to discern
a corner here,
a crumb there—
those corners and crumbs that best respond
to the signs of the times—
signs from you, my God!

Of course,
in every generation,
to rush to the aid of your Son—
   your Son starving, naked,
   tortured, oppressed—
is:
to rush to the aid of Christ
in the Eucharist of the Poor,
today.

Injustice has mounted to such a pitch
in our day
that charity
must now mean
first and foremost
seeking justice—
without forgetting
that Justice is Love.

# What a consolation, O Lord ...

... to know
that you do not require success—
that you collect no triumphs ...

Yes, you demand we not spare ourselves,
that we give ourselves to the limit,
without self-reliance,
without vanity,
without pride,
for pride can poison all,
ruin everything ...

But it may be
that in our whole life
nothing is of more worth, in your sight,
than the serene, tranquil, happy willingness
to come to you
without a victor's glory!

# Make of me a rainbow ...

... of kindness,
hope,
and peace! ...

A rainbow
that will never lie—
never proclaim false kindness,
vain hope,
mendacious peace ...

A rainbow spread by you,
presage and promise
that these will never fail:
    your Fatherly Love,
    the Death of your Son,
    and the prodigious Action
       of your Spirit, Lord!

# Forthright and clear ...

... no shilly-shallying—
your word, O Lord, is a promise:

"Blessed are they
who surrender
to the Good News!
Those who keep it in their heart
shall be ever wise.

"For if they live by it
nothing shall be impossible for them,
and God's light
shall light their way."

Lord, how delicious it is
to surrender to your Good News—
swept up on billows of a vasty deep
and fear no drowning!

What a privilege—
and the perfect exemplar
is the Mother of your Son
and our Mother—
to be granted
to keep, to cherish
your word in our hearts!

Ever wise?
Yes, Lord,
with the beautiful meaning of Wisdom—
Sapientia—the savor of things divine!

Fulfill your word?
This is the work of your grace,
which never fails,
and of our fragility,
which to our dying breath
pursues us in this earthly clay.

But ... forgive me
my anxiety
over this magnificent reward!
What peril for our weakness
to be able to do all things!

Then receive my grateful prayer:
May your light
light the path
of us all—not only mine!
Keep, guard our steps!

**PRAYER-POEMS**

# Dom Helder Camara
# Speaks to His Flock

In April 1964 Paul VI designated as archbishop of Olinda and Recife Dom Helder Camara, then bishop auxiliary to the cardinal of Rio de Janeiro and secretary of the Brazilian Episcopal Conference. On the occasion of his installation as archbishop, Dom Helder addressed the following message to the people of his archdiocese. The text has been edited for inclusion here.

Providence has taken me by the hand
and led me to Olinda and Recife;
Pope Paul VI,
who has a deep knowledge of Latin America and Brazil,
decided that this key position of North-East Brazil
should be filled without delay.

It is a divine grace
to be able to detect the signs of the times,
to be abreast of modern developments,
to participate fully in the plan of God.
Let us examine together what is taking place....

Who am I
and who am I speaking to or trying to speak to?
I am a native of the North-East
addressing other natives of the North-East,
with eyes turned to Brazil,
to Latin America,
and to the world.
A human creature who regards himself
as brother in weakness and in sin to all human beings
of all races and all religions of the world.
I am a Christian
who addresses himself to Christians,
but with heart open, ecumenically,
to people of every creed and ideology.
A bishop of the Catholic church who comes,
in the imitation of Christ,
not to be served but to serve.

Catholics and non-Catholics,
believers and non-believers,
all of you accept my brotherly greetings:
"May Jesus Christ be praised!"

## The bishop belongs to all

Let no one be scandalized
if I frequent those who are considered unworthy and
    sinful.
Who is not a sinner?
Who can throw the first stone?
Our Lord,
charged with visiting publicans and eating with sinners,
replied that it is the sick who have need of the doctor.

Let no one be alarmed
if I am seen with compromising and dangerous people,
of the left or the right,
of establishment or opposition,
with reformist or anti-reformist,
revolutionary or anti-revolutionary,
with those of good faith or bad.

Let no one claim to bind me to a group,
so that I should consider that person's friends to be mine
and make my own that person's hostilities.
My door and my heart will be open to everyone,
absolutely everyone.
Christ died for all;
I must exclude no one from dialogue.

## Concern for the poor

It is clear that, loving everyone,
I must have special love,
like Christ,
for the poor.
At the last judgment,
we shall all be judged by our treatment of Christ,
of Christ who hungers and thirsts,
who is dirty, injured, and oppressed.

Continuing the existing work of our archdiocese,
I shall care for the poor,
being particularly concerned that poverty
should not degenerate into misery.
Poverty can and at times must be accepted generously
or offered spontaneously as a gift to the Father.
But misery is degrading and repellent;
it destroys the image of God that is in each of us;
it violates the right and duty of human beings
to strive for personal fulfilment.

It is obvious that I am thinking in a special way
of the people in the slums and the abandoned children.
Whoever is suffering in body or in spirit,
whether rich or poor,
whoever is desperate,
shall have a special place in the heart of the bishop.

But I do not wish to deceive anyone,

as though a little generosity and social assistance
were sufficient.
Without a doubt there are spectacular miseries
that give us no right to remain indifferent.
Often the only thing to do is to give immediate help.
However, let us not think that the problem
is limited to certain slight reforms
and let us not confuse
the good and indispensable notion of order,
the goal of all human progress,
with caricatures of it
that are responsible for the persistence of structures
that everyone recognizes cannot be preserved.

If we wish to tackle the roots of our social evils,
we must help our country to break the vicious circle
of underdevelopment and misery.
Some people are scandalized
that this should be our primary problem.
Others question the sincerity of our motives....

It would be scandalous and unforgivable
if the church were to abandon the masses
in their hour of greatest need;
they would think we had no interest in helping them
to achieve a degree of human and Christian dignity
and to raise themselves to the category of people.

## Human values to be developed

We are all convinced
that all human beings
are children of the same heavenly Father.
Those who have the same father are brothers and sisters;
let us treat one another as brothers and sisters.

We are all convinced
that God made human beings
in God's own image and likeness
and entrusted to them the mission
of dominating nature and completing the work of
    creation.
Let us do everything possible
or impossible
that work in the North-East
may be truly a participation
in the work of our Creator.

We are all convinced
that freedom is a divine gift
that must be preserved at any price.
Let us liberate,
in the fullest sense of the word,
every human creature in our midst.

We are all convinced
that our ideal
is the development of each and every creature among us.

There are not lacking today
examples of religious indifference and atheism
among highly-developed nations.
Our own development project does not seek to exclude
   God.
The more we progress materially,
the greater will be our need of a strong, clear faith
capable of illuminating from within
the construction of the new North-East....

The church has no wish to dominate the course of events.
The church is here to serve human beings,
to help them be free.
And the church will be ready to affirm
that this process of liberation,
that begins in time,
cannot be fully accomplished until the end of time,
the true beginning when the Son of God returns.

You will have noticed
that the North-East is at once
a national problem
and a center of international attention.

But the image that is presented of us,
both at home and abroad,
is invariably false.

# The world looks to the North-East

By now the North-East is a cliché,
a slogan.
The North-East does not accept this standardization of
   misery,
and cannot, must not,
accept classification as the most explosive area
of Latin America.

Let us be united in making the North-East
an anticipation of tomorrow's Brazil,
of the future Latin America,
and of the new face of the Third World.
Let us be united
because no authentic development
can be restricted to one group or to one class.
Either the entire region is developed,
with all its human groupings,
or development is distorted.

It is for this reason that I do not just appeal
to management and workers,
to rich and poor,
to left and right,
to believer and non-believer,
that they should agree on a truce.
It is essential to begin,
trustingly,
a crescendo of dialogue.
It would be a grave matter

before the judgment of God and of history
to withdraw oneself
from the reconstruction of the world.

As part of Brazil and Latin America,
we bear the responsibility of being the Christian portion,
the Christian continent,
of the Third World.
Clearly we do not claim to be superior or better
than our Asian and African brothers and sisters.
But we have greater responsibility....

## Christ is José, Antonio, Severino

Let us press on without delay with the task of
    development
as a Christian means of evangelizing.
What value can there be in venerating pretty images of
    Christ,
or even recognizing his disfigured face in that of the poor,
if we fail to identify him with human beings
who need to be rescued from their underdeveloped
    condition.

However strange it may seem to some,
Christ in the North-East is called
José,
Antonio,
Severino ...
Behold the man!
This is Christ,
the person who needs justice,

who has a right to justice,
who deserves justice.
If we are to avoid sterile and destructive violence
on the part of the oppressed,
we must look beyond the appearance of harmony
that makes dialogue impossible....

Everyone knows and shouts about the need
for radical reform in our country.
In the past there has been mistrust of the reformers
and the constant fear of communist infiltration.
Now that the situation has changed there is no time to
    lose.
The desired reforms must come without delay.
Let them be just and balanced,
but on no account must they give
the impression of mystification.

The reforms should come in a spontaneous way and,
above all,
without rancor or ill-feeling.
Let the Brazilian people be incapable of hatred,
realizing that this is the greatest sin,
since God is charity,
God is love.

As for the North-East,
which begins its development
against a background of depressions and hopes,
let it be an example to the whole country

of a dynamic peace founded on justice,
of truth rooted in charity,
of dialogue and understanding that transcend divisions
capable of dragging the country into civil war and chaos.

Let the North-East be an example to the whole of Brazil
of a speedy recovery from political crisis.
Without prejudice to national security measures
of vigilance towards communism,
let us not accuse of communism
those who simply hunger and thirst for social justice
and the development of our country.
Let us help Brazil not to destroy the hopes of the people.

We shall prove that democracy is capable of tackling
the very roots of our social evils....

Instead of trying to reform others,
let us first reform ourselves.
The difference between the pharisees and the saints
is that the pharisees are big-hearted with themselves
and strict with others,
trying to force them into heaven.
Saints are rigorous only with themselves;
with sinners they are as generous as the goodness of God,
boundless as the mercy of the Father....

## The time of ecumenism

Being moved still by the spirit of the council,
we encourage all our people to keep in mind at all times
—in our meetings,
in our studies,
in our prayer
—not only those of other religions,
but also those who are unaffiliated to any church.
I have a particular regard for people of no faith,
who wander in darkness,
especially when they are atheist in name but Christian in
    deed.

To those who constitute "the world," as we call it,
I repeat the inspired words of Paul VI:
"Let the world know that the church looks on it
with profound understanding,
with sincere admiration,
and with the genuine intention not of conquering it,
but of serving it;
not of despising it,
but of appreciating it;
not of condemning it,
but of strengthening and saving it."

The devout who hear my words
are probably thinking that their bishop
is more concerned with the strayed sheep
than with the ninety-nine who never abandoned the flock.

But isn't this precisely the attitude
of the Good Shepherd?

Obviously we shall have time also
for our revered and devoted faithful.
Our work with them will be inspired
by the transfiguration of the Lord,
the title of our archdiocese:
by our baptism we are made one with Christ.
Instead of a worn and faded Christ,
it is necessary that he be transfigured in us
as he was on Mount Tabor.
Our Lady,
patroness of Olinda and Recife,
will assist in the glorification of her Son
in and through us.

Do you remember the moving spectacle
at the death of Pope John XXIII?
This unforgettable scene is,
I am sure,
lesson for all of us.
Catholics and non-Catholics,
believers and non-believers,
people of all races, creeds, and ideologies
suffered with the pope in his last agony
and lamented his death
as the death of a father,

thereby manifesting the implicit desire of the people:
a prelate,
a bishop must be good like Pope John.

Pray to your heavenly Father,
the giver of every grace and every light,
that this may be the livery of your new bishop;
that he may remind you of Pope John XXIII.
This will be an excellent way of reminding you
of Christ himself,
the Good Shepherd.